"Y'all Are Rude!" Too

Mind Your Manners

With Miss Lora

By Miss Lora

"Y'all Are Rude Too!"

Mind Your Manners With Miss Lora

ISBN-13: 978-0692059623

ISBN-10: 0692059628

She Speaks Publishing

People are really talking about Miss Lora with her TV appearances on the National TV Show "The List" and her "Y'all Are Rude!" book and webseries at MissLora.com. Find her at facebook.com/AskMissLora2, on Twitter @AskMissLora and on YouTube under Miss Lora:

"Miss Lora, you're smart and funny! I need you around all the time!"

"I love Miss Lora and it's just great to see you on TV telling people how not to be rude! I just feel good after I watch you"

"I actually did what you advised in one of your videos recently to some rude people and it worked! The Trailer Trash Miz Manners knows what she's talking about!"

"I LOVE the Miss Lora videos. I still laugh every time I say to someone: "People are just rude, rude, rude!"

"I started saying and tweeting to people "Y'all are rude!" and I'm not even from the South but it works!"

"After Miss Lora, baking soda will never be the same!"

"Miss Lora, you make me laugh every time I see you on "The List" – keep it up!"

"I love Miss Lora! I share you with everyone I know!"

"Miss Lora for President! Yea!"

"Keep that advice coming, Miss Lora – we need it!

"Miss Lora, I look forward to every episode!"

"Miss Lora, I laugh almost as much at the baking soda tips as I do your advice. Can't wait to see your next episode on TV!"

"Thanks, Miss Lora, your advice nails it right on the head!"

"I'm a Bubba and I love your videos!"

"There's one word for you, Miss Lora, - great!"

Acknowledgements

Thank you to everyone at the Nationally Syndicated TV Show "The List" who have made me feel so welcome including Co-Executive Producer Abbie Smith and Executive Producer Tracy Mazuer, Hosts Kristina Guerrero and Donna Ruko, Producer Meredith Witthar and Senior Producer Dave Taylor, Angie Waters whose makeup magic makes even me look good and a special Thanks to Host Extraordinaire Lindsey Granger who fills these episodes with joy and laughter and makes them so much fun to do!

Many thanks to my Momma and Daddy for their love and advice, for teaching me manners and how to talk to total strangers about anything. Really.

To my sisters Diana and Virginia who taught me everything I needed to know about sharing, fighting, negotiating, working it out and having fun. You are such beautiful women. Thank you Diana for being my biggest cheerleader always!

Thank you too to the referee skills I learned due to the countless children and adults that lived with us while we were growing up because of the boundless generosity of my parents' huge hearts who always found a space somewhere for anyone who needed it.

Utter gratitude to Sonia Barrett who has supported me in ways I can't begin to count including watching more episodes of my webseries and TV shows than she ever wanted to because I was too afraid to look and editing my books and articles. You are the best and long may we laugh!

Huge thank you to PJ Gaynard, who directed and produced my webseries and to Lillian Fidler who designed MissLora.com and my book covers.

Thanks to my amazing friends who have encouraged Miss Lora to speak out loud where everybody could hear her: Laura, Lynne, Ken, Ava, Joy, Bobby, Don, Linda, Lavender, Alison, Connie, Sherrie, Kelli, Bethanne, Kym, Judith and so many more.

Gratitude to my teachers who have totally believed in Miss Lora and all my comedy and writing coaches who said "Just be you!"

Thanks to Rachael Ray, CNN and all the radio and TV people I have worked with over the years and the audiences who let me babble, babble, babble.

And a big ole thanks to God for letting me grow up in the South, swimming with gators and learning how to make the world a better place by bossing everyone around about being more polite. It's a calling in a world of rudeness and I thank you for it. Really.

TABLE OF CONTENTS

INTRODUCTION

Dating & Relationships

Dating & Cussing - pg. 2

No Yodeling & Dating - pg. 4

Grocery Dating No No's - pg. 6

Rude Bride & Good Gift - pg. 8

Work & Jobs

Bad Bosses & Baking Soda - pg. 12

Coworkers & Feet - pg. 14

Kids & Family

Videogames & Girlfriends - pg. 18

Ipads & Parenting - pg. 20

Kid Swim & Green Hair - pg. 22

Neighbors

Bubba & Baggy Pants - pg. 26

Bubba Trouble - pg. 28

Pets

Dog People Unite - pg. 32

Cat People Unite - pg. 34

Fashion

Fashion & the Donut Monster - pg. 38

Big Ole Purses - pg. 40

Driving

Walmart & Bad Drivers - pg. 44

Rude Texting & Driving - pg. 46

Communication

Rude Words & Church - pg. 50

Compliments, Bless Yer Heart! - pg. 52

Life

Rude Gym & Weight Lifting - pg. 56

Flying & Fees - pg. 58

"The List" TV Episodes

Pg. 62 – 88

Baking Soda Tips

Tips 1 – 21 - pg. 90 - 99

Your Baking Soda Tips - pg. 100 - 102

Introduction

Well howdy, I'm Miss Lora and it's several years later and guess what? Y'all Are still Rude! Actually the whole world has gotten ruder, ruder, ruder which is probably why I ended up on a Nationally syndicated TV Show like "The List" because now we Really need tips on manners and etiquette.

I've become a regular expert for the show where everything under the sun is given to you in list of tips (hence the name) and if you'd like to find out more about the show and where it airs, you can check out www.TheListTVShow.com. I'd also love to hear from you directly and you can keep up with my episodes and posts on www.facebook.com/AskMissLora2 and on Twitter @AskMissLora

It's been an eventful time for the Trailer Trash Miz Manners after I decided everybody needed a Southern manners expert born and raised to teach y'all how to be more polite. My Youtube webseries "Y'all Are Rude!" got over a million and half views and even an appearance on the Rachael Ray CBS TV talk show.

Next, I hosted my own internet TV talk show called "Civil Wars" where my round table of journalistic experts talked about the craziness of the world in general and interviewed Hollywood and entertainment celebrities. Then I had several networks interested in my reality show and was picked up by "The List" who decided to join the battle against the epidemic of Rudeness by giving the world my dead on advice with more common sense than a stampeding herd of rabid possums (which is what people are still acting like most of the time).

Now I've compiled the best of my "Y'all Are Rude" advice with the webseries insights and laughs and all the TV episodes from "The List" plus those great tips on baking soda too in my new book "Y'all Are Rude Too!" ! I still believe baking soda can save the world from dirt and disorder (and stink – baking soda and peroxide will take the skunk right off of you) and I can save the world from rudeness and rancor and all the people that are Rude, Rude, Rude!

So if your life still isn't going the way you want, it may be cuz you're actin' just plain obnoxious. But that's okay cuz I can fix that. Just check out the advice in my book that's based on real problems from folks just like you! Then let me help you with your rude situations! Just write me at MissLora@MissLora.com, check out my website at www.MissLora.com and at Miss Lora on Youtube. Plus we can talk directly on www.facebook.com/AskMissLora2 and Twitter @AskMissLora. And remember, mind your manners, y'all!

DATING & RELATIONSHIPS

Dating & Cussing

When it comes to dating, Y'all Are Rude! I got a letter from Beth Anne and she said,

"Miss Lora, I finally decided to take your advice and get on one of those Internet dating sites. I exchanged a couple of emails with a gentlemen. When it came time for the phone call, pretty much everything that came out of his mouth were cuss words. My first thought was, oh how rude. And then I wasn't sure if he was nervous or just stupid. So I got off the phone and didn't make a date with him and now he wants me to call him back. What do I do?"

Oh honey, you just brought up one of Miss Lora's pet peeves when it comes to men and dating and that is cussing. Cuz gentlemen, you don't want to go there, trust me. You're talking to a lady and she doesn't want to hear that crap. You've got one chance to make a good impression and when she jumps off that phone without makin' a date with you, it's probably because of that potty mouth. Really. Now I know a lot of you men are probably sayin', "But, Miss Lora, I'm just being me". Well, how's that working for you, hon?

So cut out the cussing. Try a dictionary. Try a thesaurus. Try usin' the words extraordinary, magnificent, and robust in a sentence every once in a while. Now that'll make you sound like a catch. Because when you say, "Hey baby, you've got a pretty mouth and BLEEEEEEEEEEP!"; what you really want to say is, "You sure have a pretty picture and I'd like to take you for a steak dinner at Denny's." Really.

Baking Soda Tip

Now, here's another tip. Bad language often goes with bad breath but I've got a solution for that: baking soda, hon, really. Just take about a half teaspoon of this with a little glass of water to wash your mouth out because you probably need to. Swallow it down and you'll have sweet breath to impress some nice girl. Well, at least, til another cuss word comes flyin' out of your mouth. Mmhmm. Until next time, mind your manners, y'all.

No Yodeling & Dating

When it comes to first impressions on a date, Y'all Are Rude! Everybody knows I'm always talkin' about how important it is to act right when you first meet somebody. My number one no no? Cussing. And now, thanks to Emma Lou's letter, I have a new number two: yodeling. Umhmm. Honey, I had to call her for this one. She said,

"I met this guy on the internet and we decided to meet downtown for coffee. And in front of God and everyone, he greeted me with "Yodelayheehoooo".   I was stunned speechless. So what did he do? He did it again. What did he expect me to do? Yodel back?"

Actually, Miss Lora has a little empathy for this guy because, well, I have been known to impress quite a few gentlemen with my hog-calling abilities. But I never did it on a first date and certainly not in public. That's fourth date activity, if you know what I mean and I think you do. Then things got even worse for Emma Lou. He stuck his hands under her elbows and lifted her straight up and then said, "Oh, I guess you do weigh 125 pounds like you said in your ad."

Well honey, as you can guess, that date was over right then and there. He was just lucky that she didn't kick him somewhere sensitive because he just lifted up a total stranger and then weighed her like a side of beef. You've got to at least buy us dinner before you get to experience magic like that. Really.

Baking Soda Tip

Now if you want to make a good first impression every time, all you need is baking soda, hon, really. Just sprinkle a little bit of this in your facial soap and then gently scrub your face. It will get rid of all that grease and dead skin. You'll look all smooth and shiny and pretty and make a wonderful impression on your date - unless you start yodeling. Until next time, mind your manners, y'all.

Grocery Dating No No's

When it comes to dating pickups, Y'all Are Rude! Well, Danny Joe wrote in and asked,

"I've heard that grocery stores are a great place to pick up women. What's your advice?"

Well hon, it's like a lot of things in life. It depends on where you do it and how you do it. If you're gonna chase a woman all around the grocery store, that's just rude. And you definitely don't want to start up a conversation in the feminine products section. Trust me. But what Miss Lora does approve of is the produce department.

Now don't be stalking her at the celery or standing provocatively at the bananas. And for heaven's sake, don't squeeze the melons. You may think that's sexy but we just think you're grabby and maybe you can't keep your hands off anything else either. So just ask her for a suggestion about the lovely squash you have in your hands. Or maybe you can talk to her about a dish that you've come up with and strike up a conversation because all women know that a man that cooks is a keeper.

Now here's a major tip. Only hit on the women who are all dolled up. Cuz if you hit on a girl that comes in there in some Hello Kitty pajamas and is holding a quart of ice cream, she is having a bad day. Well, nothin's impossible but chances are pretty slim and that means no date for you.

Baking Soda Tip

So, if you'd like your vegetables to be as fresh as you are, gentlemen, there's a perfect way to do that: baking soda, hon, really. You just sprinkle a little bit of this on your fruit and veggies and then you can scrub off all those pesticides and that waxy residue. And then they'll be perfect for making a nice dinner for your new date. Until next time, mind your manners, y'all.

Rude Bride & Good Gift

When it comes to brides, Y'all Are Rude! Did you see the article about this girl who got a lovely gift basket of food items for a wedding present? Then she asked for the receipt so that she could take it back! Then she texted the girl who gave it to her and said,

"You should have given me cash because the plates at the wedding dinner cost a hundred bucks a pop!"

Honey, this girl needs to go in the Rude Hall of Shame! In case no one ever told ya, it's not our job to pay for your wedding. That's between you and your relatives. And if y'all don't have enough money for that, there's a solution: Justice of the Peace and a pot luck in your backyard! Bet you would be grateful for that food basket then.

Look, times are tough and we're all doin' the best that we can. Our job is to say "thank you" or "thank you so much". If you don't like your present, just do the time honored thing of rewrappin' it and givin' it to someone else for Christmas - or sell it on Craigslist! Whatever - just be grateful you got anything.

Now, Miss Lora's always welcome wedding present is a gift certificate from one of those home improvement stores. And you'll end up with a free dinner for yourself cuz the newlyweds will want you to come over and ooh and ah at everything they did with your gift.

Baking Soda Tip

Now if you want to make the perfect wedding present, you tape that gift certificate to a bag of baking soda, hon, really. It's perfect for scrubbing all those greasy pots and pans and you want to get your husband in the kitchen doing dishes as early in the marriage as you can. Train him right, girls! Until next time, mind your manners, y'all.

WORK & JOBS

Bad Bosses & Baking Soda

When it comes to bosses, Y'all Are Rude! I got a letter from Jim who said,

"My boss is Rude Rude Rude! He calls me in for meetings and goes on and on about nothing! By the time I get out of there, I'm so mad I want to spit!"

Well hon, you don't want to go there, trust me, cuz spittin' is rude. And your boss? He just sounds like he's obnoxious! I can identify cause I had a boss like that. I used to work in radio. He'd call me in to listen to tapes of me and tell me that I used the word "and" wrong. And, I would ask him, "And, how do you use the word "and" wrong?" He never had an answer for that. I finally realized, you know what, he just likes to hear himself talk.

So I brought in a yellow legal pad. I started writin' down everything he said like he had the Keys to the Kingdom! When he saw that, he started preachin'! And I started writin' even more and then, it was like he was doing the Sermon on the Mount! I expected that man to turn wine into water any minute! Well guess what? My meetings got much shorter after that, mmhmm. Of course after I got out of those meetings, I'd just rip that paper off, crumple it up in a ball and throw it in the garbage. Two Points!

Baking Soda Tip

If you have a boss who's giving you an ulcer, I have a simple solution for you – baking soda, hon, really! You just take about a half a teaspoon of it in a glass of water with a valium and that'll calm everything right down. Of course, tuning out your boss' voice - that just takes practice. Until next time, mind your manners, y'all!

Coworkers & Feet

When it comes to coworkers, Y'all Are Rude! Suzie P wrote me and said,

"As part of our job, everyone in my office has to go to a networking breakfast once a month. The first thing my co worker does when she gets there is sit down, take off her shoes and then in front of God and everyone, starts rubbing her feet! Really. It's bad enough that it's a business meeting but she also has ugly feet".

Well honestly, hon, I don't know if it's possible to find anyone's feet attractive at 7am when you haven't even had your coffee yet! But you're right, she's rude cuz business and bare feet don't mix! And there's nothing like a big ole bunion to put you right off your bacon and biscuits. But I have to admit, I do feel a little sorry for her cuz some of us are just not born with pretty feet. Miss Lora has toes that are so long they look like fingers and sometimes when I wear sandals, I scare myself. Trust me.

Now Suzie needs advice to get this woman's hands off her feet and to put her clod hoppers back on. But honey, that's what God made bosses for. When coworkers are gross or obnoxious, that's what they get paid the big bucks for – to tell their employees to stop that crap! So run on over to your boss and get them to do their job and then just be thankful that she's not baring her bunions every day in the office!

Baking Soda Tip

Now if you've got a foot problem, Miss Lora has the solution – baking soda, hon, really! If you've got toenail fungus or athlete's foot, just mix a quarter cup of baking soda with an eighth of a cup of hydrogen peroxide in a small basin. Soak your doggies every night for a week or two and they'll be good as new. Until next time, mind your manners, y'all!

KIDS & FAMILY

Videogames & Girlfriends

When it comes to videogames, Y'all Are Rude! Our letter is from Sue Ellen who said,

"My boyfriend and I are both 20 years old, in college and live with our parents. He invited me to come over and have dinner that his Momma made. When I got there, he'd taken our plates and put them on the desk and said he was going to play a video game and I could just sit there and eat and watch. Then he said he was going to finish in his bedroom and I could just watch TV with his Momma. She apologized for his rudeness but he didn't think he did anything wrong".

Hon, I have one question for your boyfriend: do you plan on ever getting lucky again in this lifetime? Cuz that's some rude behavior that will make sure you never do, trust me.

Look, Miss Lora loves videogames too. She's even the voice on one of the Fall Out games. But the bottom line is, you gotta give a woman what she needs: your time, your attention and chicken wings don't hurt either. But what you really ought to have done is bought a second controller, decorated it all up, painted it and put little stickers on it. And then the two of you could play together.

Baking Soda Tip

And if you're looking for some bonus points, you could go on over to her house and scrub her kitchen with baking soda, hon, really! Cuz nothing says you're more manly than going over to your woman's Momma's house and scrubbing her kitchen sinks. And when your girl sees those muscles just glistenin' with sweat – oh honey, big plans ahead! Until next time, mind your manners, y'all!

Ipads & Parenting

When it comes to parenting stress, Y'all Are Rude – to yourselves! I got a letter from Rachel Lynn and she said,

"Miss Lora, I know you talk about the importance of relaxing in a nice hot bath with baking soda but my kids bug me so much I'm never able to take one".

Well, hon, that's what God made DVD's for... and cable... and computers and the Ipad. And if you think they're too young, my girlfriend has a 6 month old who loves playin' on the Ipad. She'll sit there for two hours next to that bathtub, playin' this app that's a doorbell. Really. Ding dong, ding dong. Of course, my girlfriend never knows when anyone is comin' to visit but that's the price you pay. What are you gonna do?

Now when I was growin' up, my Momma had 4 kids and a 4 am wake up call. So the two hours after we got home from school, we were not to bother her on the threat of death. And that was, unless you were dyin', you would be when she got her hands on ya, trust me. That was her time to do whatever she wanted including taking a bath and she was one of the happiest Mommas around.

Baking Soda Tip

Let's be honest. Maybe the real reason why you're not gettin' in the tub is cuz the kids have been in it and it's filthy with that big old black ring. You need to give them baking soda, hon, really so they can clean it out for you! Use it cuz it's organic, it's healthy and it accomplishes several things. First of all, they get exercise cuz they're in there just scrubbin' away. Then you give them 50 cents which they can run out and use for the ice cream truck! Ding dong, ding dong! And while they're out there gettin' that ice cream, you hop in the tub! Until next time, mind your manners, y'all!

Kid Swim & Green Hair

When it comes to little kids and swimming, Y'all Are Rude! In her letter, Eileen said,

"My 8 year old daughter has taken lessons the last two summers at the community pool but she still can't swim and the other kids are making fun of her. What can I do?"

Well hon, little kids can be rude, rude, rude! They used to call Miss Lora "pancake" when she was young cuz she was so skinny and flat chested. Uh huh. As for the pool, I guess you could do it kinda like my Momma and Daddy did. They'd toss me back and forth and then toss me in the water and yell, "Swim, hon, swim!". My Daddy was a fireman and he'd say, "I can resuscitate you for up to 5 minutes!"

But they have child protective laws against that now so you probably don't wanna go there, trust me. Well, here's what I did for my 8 year old. I invited over the boy she had a crush on. He got in that pool and suddenly in thirty seconds, she knew how to swim! Because no girl is going to let a boy beat her at anything – especially a cute one!

Baking Soda Tip

Well, the only part I didn't like about swimming, besides the drowning part, was that it made you look like an alien. Your hair would be puffed out to here and all green. But I have the perfect solution for that - baking soda, hon, really! Just put a little bit in your favorite shampoo. It'll strip that nasty old chlorine out of your hair and leave it all shiny and pretty and you'll be ready for your date with your crush! Until next time, mind your manners, y'all!

NEIGHBORS

Bubba & Baggy Pants

When it comes to neighbors, Y'all Are Rude! Miss Lora is having her own problem with her neighbor Bubba. He's in the trailer next door and every time I turn the lights on to do some filming for my webseries, he comes bangin' on my door askin' for a quart of oil or a beer or some baking soda. He just wants to nose in on my videos or even worse, me, (like I can avoid it).

Oh, he's not that bad. He's just a good old boy and he's got one of them piece of crap Chevy up on concrete blocks in his front yard. He's been workin' on it for decades. Every weekend, he's out there with the hood up and him bent over the engine with his pants down to here and the moon shining where I don't want to see it. Has he never heard of a XXL tee shirt to cover that stuff? Really.

But he's not the only one. What is it about these young men who have all got their pants down to here and their underwear up to there? And you girls aren't any better with your thongs hanging out of your jeans. I mean please - get a belt, get a clue! Because y'all are rude and your underwear aren't that interesting. Although I have to admit anything would be better than looking at Bubba's butt crack. Really. But honey, until he gets that Chevy fixed, I'm doomed to the moon.

Baking Soda Tip

Now, if you want to make your automobile better, I got a solution for that: baking soda, hon, really! You just mix some water with it and make a paste. Then you spread it all over your battery connectors and cables and it will bubble up and clean off that nasty old corrosion without any scrubbing at all. Until next time, mind your manners, y'all.

Bubba Trouble

When it comes to gettin' along with the neighbors, Y'all Are Rude! Oh Lord, there's trouble in the trailer park and I'm right in the middle of it. I got this card from Miss Irene. She lives on the other side of Bubba, my next door neighbor. He's the one with the beat up Chevy on blocks and the butt crack. Mmhmm. Well, Miss Irene said,

"Bubba and the boys like to sit out in front of their trailer every weekend till the wee hours, being loud and drinking and smoking and playing cards. What should I do?"

Well, then I got a letter from Bubba, on newspaper, no less. He said,

"Miss Irene is rude, rude, rude. She's always yellin' about us bein' loud and then she turns the sprinklers on us! She is violatin' our sacred man time!"

Now, normally, my sympathy would be with Miss Irene because we're women and we girls got to stick together except that there are some extenuating circumstances. Just between you and me, I go over every other weekend and play cards with Bubba and the boys. And the drunker and rowdier they get, the more money I win. Really. And you don't want to be interferin' with Miss Lora's revenue, trust me. So I need to referee.

Now Miss Irene loves to bake and she always has leftovers from the church pot lucks. I propose she make brownies and snacks for the boys. In exchange, they give her ear plugs and a little sip of their favorite hooch so that she can sleep better at night. Plus, they'll make a concentrated effort to be a little quieter after eleven. That way, Miss Irene gets her beauty sleep, which heaven knows she needs, and me? I get to keep fleecin' those boys for every dime they've got. Really.

Baking Soda Tip

Well, if you'd like to make your life better, all you need is baking soda, hon, really. Just take about a half a teaspoon of baking soda and put it in any recipe of your baked goods. It'll make them rise better and taste better and then you can convince yourself that you're doing somethin' healthy while you're eatin' all that crap. Until next time, mind your manners, y'all.

PETS

Dog People Unite

When it comes to other people's dogs, Y'all Are Rude! My friend Verna has her dog Captain Awesome, yeah I know, ridiculous name. Anyway she had to tie him up outside the Quicky Mart so she could go in and get him some water. When she came out, there was this crazy lady with Captain Awesome in her arms. She then gave Verna a hand written note that said "You deserve a one million dollar fine for not taking care of your pet".

Well, I think she deserved a punch in the nose from Verna for being rude cuz honey, you don't touch somebody else's dog! Really. I don't even reach down to pet one unless I say "Is it ok? Do they like people?" But I don't know what's worse: people being rude to other people's dogs or being rude to their own. I was walking down the street the other day and I saw this cute little baby stroller. I leaned down to take a peek and what do you think it was? A dog.

I love animals but I don't understand these people that treat dogs like humans, like my Grandma for instance. She had seven kids and she treated 'em all like crap. Once they moved out, she got this dog who was king of the castle at her house. He even ate at the dinner table with them. Oh, I know you're thinkin', I like to sneak snacks under the table to my dog too. No honey, that's not what I'm talkin' about. This dog had its own high chair, plate, and place mat. If my Grandma could have taught that dog how to use a fork and knife, she woulda done it. Really.

But truthfully, there is nothin' more disgusting then sitting at the dinner table next to a Shitzsu with the dog fur flying all over the place and the dogs' face buried in its plate, slurpin' and chompin' on the same chicken fried steak that you are. Nasty. I finally had to tell my momma that I didn't care how good my grandma's cooking was; I wasn't coming over till y'all started playing cards. Really.

Baking Soda Tip

Now, if you'd like to do something nice for your dog, I've got a solution for that: baking soda, hon, really. Just put some of this in their doggy shampoo and you know those little itchy hot spots they get? It'll clear them right up and their fur will be perfect for petting after that. But keep 'em on the floor and off the dining room table and chairs, I'm beggin' you. Until next time, mind your manners y'all.

Cat People Unite

When it comes to cats, Y'all Are Rude! I knew that the minute I mentioned my friend Verna's dog, Captain Awesome, mmhmm, that I'd hear about cats. So I got a letter from Johnny Lee and he said,

"I've been dating this nice girl from work. She finally invited me over but when I got there, it was a studio apartment with seven cats! In a five hundred square foot space, it was cats gone wild! There were cats on the couch, cats on the kitchen counter, and don't even get me started on those kitty litter boxes. Really".

Johnny Lee got that one from me, of course. Anyway, now truth to tell, he's kind of afraid to go back. I can't really blame him cuz that girl's got some serious cat lady syndrome. Now look, Miss Lora loves cats. I have never gotten over the loss of my beloved Leo. We were together for sixteen years. He was a big, fat, fluffy orange Tabby and between my hair and my nails, we kind of matched.

He was a good old boy, but he could never get enough attention. I used to have to beg people to come over to my house just to pet my kitty. Really. But now he's in an urn on a shelf with pictures of him and his favorite pet toys. Oh, I know what you're thinkin' – that it's too much. Well, the bottom line is that I slept in the same bed with that cat longer than anybody else and he deserves some respect!

But when it comes to dating advice, I believe there is a mathematical formula to cat ownership. It's kinda like what they do with elevators where there's not supposed to be more than 10 occupants to a space. Anymore than two cats per occupant and that means no gettin' lucky for you. So, Johnny Lee, you've got to give this woman a choice: it's either kitty pettin' or heavy pettin'.

Baking Soda Tip

Now, if you want to do something nice for your kitties, all you need is baking soda, hon, really. Just take about a cup of this – oh, what am I talkin' about, you just need to dump the whole HUGE bag of it into that kitty litter box and pray for the best. Really. Until next time, mind your manners, y'all.

FASHION

Fashion & The Donut Monster

When it comes to fashion, Y'all Are Rude! I got a letter from Eddie and he said,

"Miss Lora, you gotta save me! My wife keeps asking me that dreaded question: do I look fat in this? If I say No, then she starts yelling that she is too fat! If I say Yes, then I'm on the couch for a week! Please help me!"

Well, hon, your wife is rude, rude, rude as is any woman who asks a man that question. The truth is, that even though you have that crazy voice running around in your head doesn't mean that you should ever let it out. Because the next thing you know, you could be standin' on top of your trailer, eatin' a box of doughnuts, breathin' fire like some crazy monster! Men live in terror of this every day. Really.

The bottom line is that fashion is dictated by little European men who got no hips and no butt. Now there may be a few women who look like that but come on, we're Americans. We eat crap – and a lot of it. The only thing you men ought to be sayin' is "You look lovely, hon". That'll keep the Doughnut Monster away!

Baking Soda Tip

Well, if you ladies want to look pretty all the time, I've got the perfect solution for you: baking soda, hon, really. You just sprinkle a little bit of it on the toothpaste on your toothbrush and your pearly whites will be gleamin' so much, nobody will even notice if you're fat. Really. Until next time, mind yer manners, y'all!

Big Ole Purses

When it comes to purses, Y'all Are Rude! See, me and my crazy friend Verna went to the convenience store to pick up some beef jerky and Twinkies. You know, dinner. Hey, it's an entree and dessert, deal with it. Anyway, after wanderin' around the store, we were standin' at the cash register when some guy shoved me from behind. I turned around ready to fight and he said,

"You hit me with your purse - twice!".

I realized, oops, guilty as charged and said I was sorry. But he wouldn't even accept my apology and he just stomped off! Ok, I know that the fashion rule of thumb is you're never supposed to carry a bag bigger than your butt. But for some of us, that means a really big bag. You have to understand that some women have a biological imperative that we have to carry every single thing for an emergency in our purses.

You need snacks for the kids to keep them quiet? I got that. You need a hangover remedy? I got that too. You need one of them all in one carpenter tools/Swiss army knives that's got a fire starter attached to it that will start a fire in two tries or less? I've got that too! You could take my purse camping and the only thing you'd need to bring is a sleeping bag and a tent – and if I could figure out how to fold them up really small, I'd get them in there too. Really.

So the next time a woman hits you with her purse, just accept her apology and be grateful . Because the next time that you lock your keys in the car, she might just be the only person within twenty five miles to have a Slim Jim in her purse to get it open for ya. Really.

Baking Soda Tip

Now ladies, you need to make sure you have the most important thing in your purse which is a zip lock baggy of mother's little helper: baking soda, hon, really. Cause if you or the kids get sunburned, you could just mix it with water and make a little paste and very gently put it on all those burned places. By the time you get home and rinse it off, the red will be completely gone! Really. Until next time, mind your manners, y'all.

DRIVING

Walmart & Bad Drivers

When it comes to bad drivers, Y'all Are Rude!   Our letter comes from Bobby Joe who said,

 "What is the problem? Every time I go to the Walmart and try to cross the parking lot, somebody speeds up their car and almost hits me with it! Don't they see me? What's up with that?"

Hon, you don't need Miss Lora to tell you that that is Rude Rude Rude! And if you're one of them drivers, y'all need to SLOW DOWN! What's the hurry? It's not like those cheap prices are goin' anywhere. They're not gonna jump off the shelf and start runnin' around like a chicken with its head cut off. That only happens occasionally on Black Friday and on that day, y'all are on your own then. Really.

Now it's not rude to yell at the drivers of those cars which is what Miss Lora did when one of 'em almost hit her last week. Well, wait a second, maybe I need to clarify. I yelled at them from the sidewalk. Cuz there are certain laws of physics that you are never ever gonna be able to change. One of them is car, big- you, small. You don't want to go there, trust me.

Baking Soda Tip

It is a stressful situation but Miss Lora has the perfect solution for it: a hot bath and baking soda, hon, really! It's organic, it's healthy and it's cheap! It's a great detoxer, gets rid of all that electromagnetic energy and clears out your auric field. I don't know what that means but it works, whatever. Anyway, some people just like to use a little bit of it but I say just dump it all in there. And if you mix it with Epsom Salts, you get these bubbles. So then when you're sittin' in the tub, you get all these little tingles. Miss Lora is a big believer that life is hard. We need to get our tingles wherever we can – especially if they're legal and cheap! Until next time, mind your manners, y'all!

Rude Texting & Driving

When it comes to texting, Y'all Are Rude! I got a letter from Sarah Lynn and she said,

"I car pool to work every day with a guy who recently started texting on his smartphone while he's driving. Now I'm terrified we're gonna have a terrible accident because not only is it rude to text while you drive, it's illegal in a bunch of states!"

Well, I can identify cuz I had a similar problem with my crazy friend Verna. She was drivin' me and all my friends around and she started textin' away on her phone. I said "Honey, you may be ok with killin' yourself but me and all my people, we're precious cargo!" So here's how I handled that. I picked up her phone and tossed it onto the back seat – try and text on that, Verna!

But honestly, I don't know why everyone is doin' it. It's not like textin' in the car is something that even matters. It's not like puttin' on make-up or shavin' - that's important stuff. Look, I know distracted driving is a big problem, especially for someone like Verna. She drives home from work every day wigglin' out of her pantyhose. How does she do that? She's small chested. What does she use to drive? Her chin?

And do you know that she was one of the first people to get a car with an electrical outlet in the dashboard? Then she bought one of those fry baby deep fryers. Now she plugs it in every single morning on her way to work and makes the doughnuts. Really. Why can't she go to the Piggly Wiggly like the rest of us? You can just see her, drivin' down the road, texting on her phone, makin' the doughnuts. Double trouble. But she never gets in any trouble. Whenever a cop pulls her over, all she has to do is roll down the window and hand over the doughnut.

Baking Soda Tip

But if you're cookin' in the car, the grease stains on the upholstery are horrendous so you need baking soda, hon, really. Just sprinkle a little bit on the spots, it will lift that grease right up. Then you take an old toothbrush and scrap it all away and it's good as new. At least, until she makes the next batch of doughnuts. Until next time, mind your manners, y'all.

COMMUNICATION

Rude Words & Church

When it comes to church, Y'all Are Rude! I was so excited recently cuz I got to sing a solo in church. The preacher said it was 'Hell and Damnation Week' so I picked Johnny Cash's song Ring of Fire. "I fell into a burnin' ring of fire, I went down, down", well, you know the rest of it. I don't have to go there. Anyway, I got some nice applause but after the service, this woman who will remain nameless (Jessica Lynn) said to me right in front of the preacher,

"That song, that was interesting".

Well, honey, she might as well have just stood up in front of the whole church and said "You stunk" because it pretty much means the same thing. And I realized that there are three words like that. No matter how you use those words, they're rude, rude, rude and "interesting" is number one.

The second one? Oh you can guess it - "whatever". Mmhmm. No matter how you say whatever, it basically has three meanings: one, you're a liar and we all know it; two, it's time for you to be quiet now because nobody wants to hear you anymore or three, basically, you can kiss my butt.

The third word is "fine". Now you men accuse us women of sayin' it all the time and you know what? You're right. We do. And depending on the tone of voice and how long we stretch out the word fine, it's gonna determine how much you're in the dog house and how many nights you're spendin' on the couch. Really.

Baking Soda Tip

Now, if you gentlemen would like to make that time on the couch a little nicer, I've got a solution for that: baking soda, hon, really. All ya gotta do is pick up them couch cushions and get all those nasty pizza crusts and Twinkie wrappers out of there. Then sprinkle a little bit of baking soda on the bottom. Vacuum it all up and it will smell good as new. And with all that cleanin', it might earn you some extra points with the Mrs. and get you off the couch that much quicker. See, that's the thing about baking soda. Whatever interesting things you do, it makes it all fine. Until next time, mind your manners, y'all.

Compliments, Bless Yer Heart

When it comes to compliments, Y'all Are Rude! Linda S. wrote me and said,

"Miss Lora, I know you talk about the importance of compliments but a woman came up to me at the Piggly Wiggly and said:"I just love that outfit you wear more and more every time I see it." What do I say to that other than (bleep)?"

Oh honey, you just entered the Rude Hall of Shame with those nasty little people who give compliments that aren't really compliments. Like: "Did you do something with your hair?" Or the even more popular: "Did you lose weight?" You could say something back like "No, hon, you just remember me as fatter". But then you'd be just as rude as them. Or you could whack 'em upside the head which is what they really deserve but that could get you jail time and you don't want to go there, trust me.

Instead, Miss Lora recommends you adopt the phrase that has stood the test of time with Southerners everywhere: bless yer heart. It turns the simplest phrase like: "How nice of you to notice my dress, bless yer heart" and translates it into "Hon, you can kiss my chunky monkey butt" or "You're an idiot but we've learned to put up with you".

And you can't beat its versatility. If you do need to express sympathy or support, just addin' it to any sentence will pretty much do the trick: "I'm sorry you caught your fiancé cheatin' on you with your best friend in your closet but at least you found out before the wedding, bless yer heart".

Baking Soda Tip

Now if you need to decontaminate your clothes, you just need baking soda, hon – really! Just add half a cup to your washer and it acts as a laundry booster to make your clothes cleaner, your whites brighter and it can even erase the stain of betrayal. Really. Until next time, mind your manners, y'all!

LIFE

Rude Gym & Weight Lifting

When it comes to the gym, Y'all Are Rude! I got a letter from Emma Kay who said,

"What is the deal with the gym? Men in there are rude, rude, rude. They take these big old weights and they put them on the machines and then they walk away and leave them!"

This is one of Miss Lora's major pet peeves. Oh, it's hard enough for me to drag my lazy butt into the gym. When I do show up, I can't use half the things in there because it has eighteen million pounds of plate on it! Do we look like we can lift this stuff? No, because we do not have the big ole arms and shoulders that you do and our center of gravity is a lot lower.

Instead, we have what are called hips. Yes, God gave us hips to carry babies and groceries, not forty-five pound plates. Course, if they made it in the shape of a purse and slapped a Birkin logo and a five thousand dollar price tag on it, we would probably manage. Huh, maybe I got me a new fashion trend. Anyway, be a gentleman and take the plates off after you work out.

Oh, and please wipe down after yourself too. There is nothing more disgustin' than sitting on one of them padded benches and slidin' right off because of all the sweat on it. Rude, rude, rude! And you women aren't off the hook either. Every time I go into an exercise class filled with women, it frankly, well, stinks because of your funky tennis shoes. I don't care how cute and pink those tennies are. The bottom line is: pink don't cover the stink.

Baking Soda Tip

Now what does cover the stink is - baking soda, hon, really. You just sprinkle a little bit of this in those funky tennis shoes and shake out the excess and they'll be smelling fine in no time. Until next time, mind your manners, y'all.

Flying & Fees

When it comes to luggage, Y'all Are Rude! Ernie D. wrote after his recent trip:

"Why is that everyone has to crowd around the luggage carousel when their suitcase is nowhere in sight and makes it impossible for us to get our big ole one out?"

You're right hon, they are rude, rude, rude cuz luggage is one of those areas where we totally violate the fashion rule of never having a bag bigger than your butt. Miss Lora's suitcase is always oversized and overweight cuz I gotta put my Twinkies somewhere.

But the bottom line is that if my hips don't fit in next to you at the carousel then my bag is definitely not going to fit coming out – not without whackin' the heck out of you cuz you won't get out of the way!

But I don't know who's ruder now – them or the airlines for what they charge us to get the bag on the plane. They've got fees for everything these days. Next time I fly, I expect to be charged in the cabin for the air I breathe. It's like (sung to Old McDonald's) with a fee over here and a fee over there, here a fee, there a fee, everywhere a fee fee, oh these airlines are bankrupting me, ee ey ee ey eeeeeee!

And the one that bugs me the most: butt room. It's like every regular seat has been replaced with child sized. For a normal sized seat, you got to pay out the whazoo! I do understand that policy in other countries.

But hon, we're Americans and we eat crap – and lots of it. Butt room ought to be in our Bill of Rights!

Baking Soda Tip

Well, we can't do much about the fees for now but you can keep your luggage in better shape with baking soda, hon, really! Just make a paste of it with some water and use a scrub brush to get all those cooties off of it cuz between the TSA and the tarmac, you have no idea where it's been! Until next time, mind your manners, y'all!

"The List" TV Episodes

**Miss Lora on The List TV Show with Donna Ruko:
Featuring Y'all Are Rude!**

Donna: Thank you very much Holly.

Teresa: See that? What you just did there, thank Holly. That is a delightful example of common courtesy, something we don't see enough of in today's world.

Donna: You're right there's just too much rudeness out there. You know what, we're so sick of it that we decided to put a stop to it all… right?

Teresa: Right

Donna: It's all about you.Ok so I'm here with Miss Lora, author of "Y'all Are Rude." Was that good?

Miss Lora: Perfect!

Donna: Cause in an English accent that'll sound funny. Y'all are rude. That sounds strange.

Miss Lora: I think it's fabulous.

Donna: But you are single-handedly cleaning up America's act because people are just too rude.

Miss Lora: Oh it's so true. Somebody's gotta take the job and I decided I better take it. So I've got four tips for you on how you can be less rude. Tip number one: drive defensively and politely. I mean it doesn't kill you to let somebody in in front of you. And the most important thing is for heaven sakes, use your turn signals!

Donna: Mmmhmm.

Miss Lora: Tip number two is say please and thank you.

Donna: The basic one, that's what everyone should know.

Miss Lora: It's so true, you'd think everybody would know it! And those two words can change your whole life. Tip number three: be ready at the checkout counter. You're bad at this aren't you?

Donna: Ohhh I'm bad— yeah.

Miss Lora: I know you are! Honey when you're going up to the register take your cell phone, put it in your purse. Get out your wallet, get out your coupons and be ready. Especially with a smile because the person at the register, they've got a tough job, trust me.

Donna: Fourth tip: keep track of your kids. But you know what's another thing I think drives a lot of people crazy is children on the airplane.

Miss Lora: Ughhh

Donna: When you've got the kicking kid behind just kicking away at the back.

Miss Lora: This just happened to me, I swear! And I literally turned around and gave them that look like — and immediately.

Both: laughter

Donna: Give us that look again. What was that look?

Arnold clip: You don't stop screwing around back there this is what I'm gonna do to you.

Miss Lora on The List TV Show with Lindsey Granger: No Rude Airplane Tips!

Lindsey: The holidays are here and travel is at an all-time high. Airplane etiquette needs to be as well. Author of "Y'all Are Rude," Miss Lora is showing us how to mind our manners in the sky. We told our Facebook community about the airplane etiquette segment and they went crazy. The first issue we're tackling, the arm rest. Blair says don't put up the armrest and sit like halfway into my seat. There are so many arm rest issues, what are the rules for the arm rests?

Miss Lora: Honey it is rude to take somebody else's seat that they've paid for and that's exactly what happens when you pull that armrest up.

Lindsey: And if you're stuck in the middle seat

Miss Lora: So the bottom line is, the arm rests belong to you.

Lindsey: Next up, windows open or closed? So this is a big deal, windows open or closed. : Like look at this Susan says closed, Ashley says open, Yaritza says closed. What do you do?

Miss Lora: You need to ask because the truth is there may be somebody who's claustrophobic and they really need that window open.

Lindsey: And if people in the row just can't agree

Miss Lora: You better hope you're in a three-seat and then there's gonna be a tie breaker!

Lindsey: Next up, headphones. So Leah says, "don't play your music so loud the entire plane can hear." So you tell me what's too loud.

Miss Lora: This is the easy one. When somebody's making a face at you like this — that mean's you're too loud.

Lindsey: Next up, food. So I don't know about you but every time I get on the plane I'm hungry.

Miss Lora: Oh yeah

Lindsey: And Lauren says don't bring a full course meal on the flight. So what can you eat?

Miss Lora: The best bet is a sandwich. But honey tuna fish is not your friend.

Lindsey: Shimmeon is super passionate about this next topic. Pulling on a head rest to get up!

Miss Lora: That is rude. If you want to get up, that's what arm rests are for. If you need help, ask somebody.

Lindsey: And finally, baggage.

Lindsey: So Gina says while exiting the plane wait for the person before you to get their bag down, I'm in a rush!

Miss Lora: Rude, rude, rude honey. I don't care whether you're in a rush, don't be jumping in front of people.

Lindsey: All in all

Miss Lora: Don't be a hog. Don't hog the seat, don't hog the floor space, don't hog the aisle space, and don't hog the bathroom.

Lindsey: Minding your manners in the sky, on the low down.

Miss Lora on The List TV Show with Lindsey Granger: Rude Food on Airlines!

Lindsey: Airlines can use some etiquette tips these days but so can fellow passengers when it comes to minding their meal manners. Etiquette expert Miss Lora is giving us the do's and don'ts of in flight dining. First up: no fast food. Now I'm sorry, I love Chick-fil-A so I brought mine on board. Is this appropriate or not appropriate?

Miss Lora: Well you know what, everybody else on the plane is gonna get upset because they don't have their fast food! And so they're going to be wanting it, or resenting you because you have it and suddenly you've smelled up their whole area.

Lindsey: And beware, fast food could lead to screaming babies.

Miss Lora: And kids lose their minds, because that smell it's like, "ooh, I need some!"

Lindsey: Alright, no fast food. Next, the softer, the better. You're trying to tell me that you've made a more appropriate airplane choice than I have?

Miss Lora: Absolutely, because I have the soft, gummy, quiet, chewy choice. You have the loud, obnoxious, crackly choice.

Lindsey: Many people find the sound of crunchy chewing annoying.

Miss Lora: There are people who have whats called "Misophonia" and they have a sensitivity to loud noises, especially things like that, "crunch crunch crunch." It drives them crazy.

Lindsey: And I've got the enormous size bag so I would really make them mad. And the final rule: cold over hot.

Miss Lora: First of all I think you're living dangerously by bringing hot soup onto a plane because if you don't spill it on you then you're probably just going to spill it on the total stranger sitting next to you.

Lindsey: Miss Lora suggests staying away from most hot foods on flights.

Miss Lora: The hot tends to smell more. What I do is I make a sandwich.

Lindsey: Just know that not all cold food is ok.

Miss Lora: I can't tell you how many people bring sushi onto a plane. People are bringing on these huge tuna rolls and everything.

Lindsey: A definite in-flight dining don't. Sensibly snacking in the sky, on the to-do list.

Miss Lora on The List TV Show with Lindsey Granger: No Rude Movie Theaters!

Lindsey: Blockbuster movies at this time of the year are full of big stars, lots of action, great stories. But if you really want to enjoy a film, the audience has got to be on their best behavior too. Lindsay Granger has movie theater etiquette at the top of the list. There's nothing worse than waiting to see a new movie just to have it ruined by someone else. So we went to etiquette expert and author of, "Y'all Are Rude," Miss Lora to learn the courtesies of the cinema. You can have a bad experience during a holiday movie?

Miss Lora: Oh honey you can have a bad experience in the movie theater all year long.

Lindsey: The first rule is all about food. Let's all admit, we've all probably snuck in some snacks a time or two.

Miss Lora: Miss Lora has to admit, there's been many a time that she's snuck a burrito in her bag.

Lindsey: A burrito?

Miss Lora: Yeah!

Lindsey: Ok so if I bring like my dad's salisbury steak and a side, is that okay?

Miss Lora: No!

Lindsey: Just don't bring in a whole meal. Keep it small, contained, and make sure you clean up.

Miss Lora: They're nice enough to sell you food when you come in here. You should be polite enough, collect your stuff, throw it in the garbage can. It's not asking a lot.

Lindsey: Next up, when it comes to phones

Miss Lora: Turn it off, completely.

Lindsey: I can't even like answer a quick phone call during the previews?

Miss Lora: No! Cause guess what, there's a lot of us that actually like the previews. We would like to watch them and pay attention to them and your phone is going to distract us the same way it will distract us during the movie.

Lindsey: (phone rings) I have to take this, excuse me. So leave the theater if you need to make a call. Alright so I left like you asked me to answer my phone. Now I'm walking back in, what are the seating rules.

Miss Lora: Well first of all remember it's dark, so crouch down a bit.

Lindsey: And walk facing toward the screen.

Miss Lora: Because you don't' want to be like you know staring right at them.

Lindsey: And if you're already seated.

Miss Lora: Move your feet back. Tripping is rude.

Lindsey: And when it comes to the armrest. Who's is it? How do you know?

Miss Lora: Well its kinda the same thing like in an airplane. Bottom line is we all got to share.

Lindsey: What if I have a large popcorn and a large drink? I need both so I'm sorry, you know I've got to smoosh my popcorn down until it fits. And the last rule, talking. So I always go with a friend or family member. So can I talk to them?

Miss Lora: No! Okay, maybe. Well how about really quietly.

Lindsey: Wow okay you heard it first from Miss Lora, you're allowed to talk in the theater. So, it's not rude.

Miss Lora: (whispers)

Lindsey: Minding your manners in the movies (Lindsey puts her feet on the seat)

Miss Lora: Rude, rude, rude.

Lindsey: is on the top of the list.

Miss Lora on The List TV Show with Kristina Guerrero: No Rude House Party Tips!

Kristina: The food is ready, the drinks are poured, now all that's missing is your party guests and your manners.

Miss Lora: Hi Kristina, come on in!

Kristina: Hi, I'm ready to party! So I went to Miss Lora, etiquette expert and author of, "Y'all Are Rude" to answer all our party protocol questions. Should I be on time, fashionably late, or maybe a little bit early?

Miss Lora: Well honey if it's a dinner party you better be on time because you don't want to be the one that ends up burning the soup course. And if it's a regular party, say it's one of those parties that's gonna be you know three or four hours, just show up whenever. Just make sure you leave when they want you to, cause there's nothing worse than going, "when are they going to go?"

Kristina: I've also been that party guest as well. Next, how do I know if I should take my shoes off or not?

Miss Lora: Most people that want you to take your shoes off they got a sign somewhere that says.

Kristina: If not, you can keep them on because sometimes the shoes can make the outfit. Now what is the rule if I bring you a gift of wine?

Miss Lora: It is not rude not to share it with your friends at the party. Honey, they can get the cheap stuff because this is your present and it ought to be saved for you stashed away in the bedroom or somewhere where nobody can get to it.

Kristina: Next, do I need to ask before I post?

Miss Lora: If it's someone you know and they post every ten seconds, no you don't it's pretty clear they want their whole life all over the internet. But if it's someone you're not quite sure it's always important to ask.

Kristina: Also weddings, baby showers, those kind of things might be more private on social media.

Miss Lora: Always good to ask.

Kristina: And when the party is over…Ok what if I brought a six-pack to the party and there's some left over, can I take it home?

Miss Lora: Rude, rude, rude. I mean if you bring a beverage to a party and there's anything left over, leave it because the host is going to need it to recover from the party that they just put on.

Kristina: Absolutely it also screams, "cheapskate, cheapskate, cheapskate!"

Miss Lora: Big time! Big time!

Kristina: Party protocol is on the low down. I'm just gonna take one more.

Lora: There you go.

Miss Lora on The List TV Show with Lindsey Granger: No Rude Halloween Tips!

Lindsey: Even though you'll be all dressed up for Halloween, that doesn't mean you can forget about your manners. So we went to Miss Lora, author of "Y'all Are Rude" for her spooky, social graces. So I didn't know there were etiquette rules to Halloween, I thought it was just like a fun free-for-all.

Miss Lora: Oh no there absolutely is! You know Halloween has turned into this multi-billion dollar holiday in America. Not just because the kids are a part of it but adults have taken it over and gone wild with it.

Lindsey: And the first rule of Halloween...

Miss Lora: So the number one thing is if you're coming to a house and there's a little you know container there with the candy always say please and thank you and if someone's handing it out to you, only take one. But if they tell you you can have more than one, you got lucky!

Lindsey: So don't go crazy. To all the kids, don't stick your hand in there and take twenty. Just take a couple. Next up... For someone like me without kids, do I have to put like a big jar of candy outside of my house?

Miss Lora: Yes you do! C'mon, it's nice.

Lindsey: You're right.

Miss Lora: Yeah because now that it's become such an adult holiday a lot of people are going away from their houses.

Lindsey: So all you have to do is leave out some candy with a sign saying, "take only one."

Miss Lora: And for ten bucks you can make a kids whole night and a couple days after that when they're trading all the candy with their friends.

Lindsey: Nothing's worse than going to a door as a kid and nobody being home and there being no candy.

Miss Lora: Rude, rude, rude.

Lindsey: And finally...

Miss Lora: Just because you have a costume on and a mask, everybody knows who you are. So if you're going to a party and you've got people like coworkers there, watch your manners people.

Lindsey: Right, you don't become a gremlin just because you dressed up like a gremlin.

Miss Lora: No, no, no because the last thing you wanna do is lose your job over a Halloween party.

Lindsey: A lot of people use that costume as a shield to go one step further than they would in real life.

Miss Lora: Mmmm you know be careful, be very very careful.

Lindsey: Beware.

Miss Lora: Be afraid, be very very afraid.

Lindsey: P's & Q's meet trick or treat (Lindsey steals all the candy!)

Miss Lora: Rude, rude, rude!

Lindsey: On the top of the list.

Miss Lora on The List TV Show with Kristina Guerrero: No Rude Tipping Tips!

Kristina: The world of tipping can be confusing but Author and Etiquette Expert Miss Lora has tips to make it easy. First Up, sometimes you have to tip even when the service isn't good.

Miss Lora: The bottom line is that you can't separate the product from the service. So if the food's good and the service is bad, guess what? You still gotta tip.

Kristina: But don't do it without letting them know that the service wasn't on point.

Miss Lora: Because you want to let them know so you can even write it on the receipt: this tip is because the food was good but the service was awful.

Kristina: But at a coffee shop, regardless of the service, you can skip it.

Miss Lora: You don't need to tip your barista. They're making good money!

Kristina: Next, more good news! She says you can skip the tip on take out!

Miss Lora: The bottom line is you're already cooking the food and it's already sitting there and if I go to a fast food place, I'm getting most of that food to take with me and nobody is expecting me to tip so why am I tipping you?

Kristina: But a delivery is different. You should tip well when they bring the food to your door.

Miss Lora: If you get a $10 pizza, give them $5. Why? Because you didn't have to put on your clothes, get in the car, use your gas and the next time that person has to deliver to your house, they'll probably get there a little bit faster too.

Kristina: And finally, keep your tips simple. Use a standard percentage but make exceptions.

Miss Lora: The range is from 10 to 20 percent normally and 15 is usually what you're supposed to do for restaurants. If they did a really great job, then you give more.

Kristina: To really reward great service, tip in cash.

Miss Lora: At restaurants, when you're paying for your meal on your credit card and you put your tip on the credit card, a lot of restaurants will pass that tip around to everybody. It does not go to your server solely. So if you've had someone who's done a really great job of serving you, pay them in cash.

Kristina: For more tipping tricks, head over to the TheListTV.com. Upping your gratuity game on the Breakdown.

**Miss Lora on The List TV Show with Lindsey Granger –
Airport Holiday Travel Tips Part 1!**

Lindsey Granger has a few travel etiquette tips to make
everyone's life easier— on the breakdown. According to
triple-A, forty eight point seven million people are traveling
for the Thanksgiving holiday. If you or any of your family is
traveling by plane, etiquette expert Miss Lora has a few
airport areas where you need to mind your manners. First up,
take it easy in the parking lot.

Miss Lora: Most people get very stressed out trying to find
the parking garage at the airport and they have good reason
why.

Lindsey: You see I haven't made it there yet.

Miss Lora: Fifty-thousand accidents. Sixty-thousand injuries
a year happen in parking garages.

Lindsey: So don't ruin your trip by starting it off with a crash.
Park on the roof if you can't find a spot in the garage.

Miss Lora: Everybody's like, "oh no, I gotta have a spot right
by the elevator." At the holidays, isn't gonna happen.

Lindsey: Miss Lora says have patience and pay attention. No
texting and driving. The next place to mind your manners is
at the check in counters. Weigh your bag at home.

Lindsey: Like go buy a scale?

Miss Lora: Yes! They're like $9.99, you put it under there,
you lift the bag. Because the bottom line is 50 pounds is 50
pounds no matter how much you squish it.

Lindsey: So don't try to pull a fast one on the ticket agent.
And if you use curbside checkin, tip the skycap.

Miss Lora: They're providing a service to you. They're
keeping it so you don't have to be in line for the electronic
check-in machine. You don't have to be in line for the bag
drop. So it's about two dollars a bag.

Lindsey: So don't go up there with ten bags and one dollar.

Miss Lora: Thank you.

Lindsey: And finally, baggage claim.

Miss Lora: Well one of the places in the airport where people can be rude, rude, rude is baggage claim.

Lindsey: And it's so annoying to me, people are always bombarding me trying to get their bag first. Miss Lora says to just relax.

Miss Lora: You need to remember, your bag's coming down and it's gonna go around and around. So if you're not right on it you will get to it.

Lindsey: And once you do get it watch out for people's toes. Don't be this guy.

Miss Lora: Also, keep your head up. I can't tell you how many times people are bent over and then the next thing you know they plow right into somebody cause they're not looking at what's in front of them when they're dragging their bag with them.

Lindsey: So your texting, talking, walking, rolling — no?

Miss Lora: No.

Lindsey: Airport etiquette tips that will glide you smoothly on your way on the breakdown.

Miss Lora on The List TV Show with Lindsey Granger: Airport Holiday Travel Tips Part 2!

Lindsey: Holiday travel can be exhausting, but rewarding once you hit your destination. Etiquette expert Miss Lora says peaceful travel is possible by avoiding a few frequent flying failures. First up, be prepared at the security checkpoint.

Miss Lora: So make you've got your boarding pass, make sure you've got your ID.

Lindsey: Sorry...

Miss Lora: And what did we talk about? Have your documents ready.

Lindsey: I know! And if you have a mobile boarding pass, make sure your brightness is turned up and your auto-rotate is turned off.

Miss Lora: So it's not flip-flopping all over the place when they're trying to look at your boarding pass on your phone.

Lindsey: Once you're past the TSA agent Lora says, "don't hog the bins."

Miss Lora: No, no, no, don't be a bin-hog.

Lindsey: I need the bin!

Miss Lora: No, no, no. One per shoe?

Lindsey: Consolidate where you can to keep the line moving. Next, keep your coffee orders short.

Miss Lora: Lindsay what's your favorite coffee to order?

Lindsey: Um if it's fall I like to add caramel. If not double macchiato extra shot, caramel crystal on top, whipped cream.

Miss Lora: Don't do that, not at the airport honey. People just got done waiting in line to try to deal with their baggage and check-in and all that good stuff. The last thing I want to do is be waiting in line for you because you've decided you need a coffee order that's a mile long.

Lindsey: Miss Lora says that most airport coffee shops are run by facility managers whose main priority is getting people in and out.

Miss Lora: Keep your order for coffee less than three adjectives.

Lindsey: And finally, be courteous at your gate.

Miss Lora: First of all, don't hog the seats. There's limited space at the gate area. So see all those bags you got taken up? Take that down.

Lindsey: No taking naps across multiple seats either.

Miss Lora: Don't hog the charging stations. You need to share the plug.

Lindsey: So how many can I charge, what's fair?

Miss Lora: A phone.

Lindsey: One?

Miss Lora: Yeah. But here's the most important thing. If you're sitting there charging your phone and you're on the phone talking to somebody will you please be quiet?

Lindsey: Avoiding frequent flying fails, on the breakdown.

Miss Lora on The List TV Show with Lindsey Granger: No Rude Regifting Tips!

Lindsey: We all wanna know what's under that wrapping paper, but that doesn't mean we'll always love it. Etiquette expert and author of, "Y'all Are Rude," Miss Lora has a solution.

Miss Lora: Some people think that regifting is rude, I'm not one of them, because I believe it's just another way of sharing the love. Cause people you love gave it to you, but you should give it to someone else that would love it more than you do!

Lindsey: But there are some rules you gotta follow. Number one, give up on the really bad gifts.

Miss Lora: There are some gifts that if you look at it you should say, "that needs to be gone." Say it's a self-help book that somebody's trying to give you a hint. We don't need those hints, I need to go to the library's bookmobile thank you very much.

Lindsey: Let's say it's a fruitcake though, what do you do with that?

Miss Lora: Oh I'm sorry, it's just a doorstop. Who eats that?

Lindsey: Oh man, no grandma, noo! But when you find a gift that you do want to give away, follow rule number two. Mark what you're regifting.

Miss Lora: When you get that gift if you're looking at it thinking, "oh no, that is definitely not staying with me," then the important thing is to put a little note on it.

Lindsey: Then put all those gifts in a box

Miss Lora: Because then you're able to go into that box, pull it out, know who it came from so you don't give it back to that person.

Lindsey: And then you have a box full of presents whenever you're in a pinch.

Miss Lora: Or which you can find things for birthdays, anniversaries, you're covered! Throw some wrapping paper on it, run on down the road.

Lindsey: Rule number three, regift to the right people.

Miss Lora: Never regift anything that your mom might be able to find out.

Lindsey: If she sees your friend with that necklace on she'll know that's the necklace she bought. Give in different groups of friends so you don't get caught. And don't always assume because you didn't use it that someone else won't love it.

Miss Lora: Something that I would like— I never used it, it sat in the cupboard for two years and I finally went, "this needs to be gone." But it turned out to be a great gift for somebody else, so you never know.

Lindsey: And the final rule. Limit your regifting, because no one wants to be known as the regifter.

Miss Lora: But if you're one of those people who says, "I don't want to do regifting anymore." There is a very simple solution to stop that.

Lindsey: What's that?

Miss Lora: Tell people what you want!

Lindsey: Isn't that rude?

Miss Lora: No, everybody wants to get you something that you want

Lindsey: So send an email or a text and let them know, the rules to regifting is on the top of the list.

Miss Lora on The List TV Show with Lindsey Granger: No Rude Gym Workout Tips!

Lindsey: Studies say gym memberships spike up to 40% in January.Everybody wants to join the gym and get fit, right?

Miss Lora: Yep, get back in there and work it off. All those pounds you put on over the holiday.

Lindsey: Etiquette expert and author of, "Y'all Are Rude," Miss Lora, says theres a code of conduct act all newcomers need to follow. First up, don't leave weights around.

Miss Lora: I think it's leaving all that heavy weight on all the machines.

Lindsey: Whether it's the bench press or leg press, bring the weight back down after you're finished using it.

Lindsey: Is there like a limit you can leave on there? 10 pounds, 20 pounds?

Miss Lora: Oh I think anything 25 pounds or under, but when it gets to those 45 pound plates we start having to really work at it.

Lindsey: The next unwritten gym rule, be neat.

Miss Lora: If you're a person that's going to sweat a lot when you're using machines and the benches and all. Bring a towel, wipe it off so we're not going to be laying in it.

Lindsey: Even if you don't break a sweat, wipe your station before and after you use it.

Miss Lora: Everybody has got colds and flus, especially in the wintertime and you don't want to be picking it up along with the whole good workout too.

Lindsey: Right it's still January so the colds are running wild. The third rule is to be mindful of your funkiness. What does that mean?

Miss Lora: Well if you're a person that's coming from a long day of work and you know you might be a little ripe there. Go ahead and take a shower in the gym, then do your workout because you don't want to be bothering everybody else with fumes.

Lindsey: Also make sure to consistently wash the clothes in your gym bag.

Miss Lora: You've got their icky, yucky, clothes that should've been laundered two weeks ago and they've left them in there and forgotten to take them out and then you're bringing them into the locker room and stinking the whole place up.

Lindsey: And finally, respect space.

Miss Lora: If you're standing so you want to look in the mirror so you can get a good look at yourself make sure there's not somebody sitting right behind you that you just blocked. Rude, rude, rude.

Lindsey: So grab your dumbbell and keep it moving. Miss Lora says to also refrain from giving unsolicited advice to other gym members.

Miss Lora: Nobody wants to hear it.

Lindsey: Refreshing yourself on the unwritten rules of the gym on the fit list.

Miss Lora on The List TV Show with Lindsey Granger: No Rude Office Parties!

Lindsey: Office parties can turn into complete chaos. You can see that in the new "Office Christmas Party" film. Etiquette expert Miss Lora is telling us how to avoid craziness and act appropriately at our next work party. The first rule, do not skip it.

Miss Lora: If they're putting out all this effort in order to have that party, you better be there. Unless you're dead. Or in the hospital. Or really really sick and they don't want you to spread that to them any way... okay, okay, okay.. there's a good enough excuse.

Lindsey: Next rule, dress smart.

Miss Lora: You can have a little holiday bling going on but if you wouldn't wear it to the office, don't be wearing it to the party. I mean guys don't be wearing a wife-beater there.

Lindsey: Next, prepare your date.

Miss Lora: Just talk about what are the safe topics, what they can and can't do. And the thing is truthfully though, if you're that worried about them you need a different date.

Lindsey: Next, please watch your boredom body language.

Miss Lora: Stand there like this, you are not going to be the hit of the party and the boss is going to notice.

Lindsey: Miss Lora says this next rule is the most important. Don't get wasted.

Miss Lora: Miss Lora's rules of thumb are: more than one, you're no fun. More than two, you could be through, trust me. Well you could be going in next Monday morning and there's no job for you left.

Lindsey: So no more than two drinks.

Miss Lora: This is the opportunity for your boss and your coworkers to get to see you in another situation and you could blow it so quickly.

Lindsey: 'Tis the season to stay employed, on the to-do list.

Miss Lora on The List TV Show with Lindsey Granger: Kids Telling Adults Y'all Are Rude!

Lindsey: Every day adults do things they tell their kids not to do. Over the summer especially rules tend to be more relaxed. Now that it's the beginning of the school year, it's time for us adults to practice what we preach. Here are three tips to help us be on our best behavior. First:

Kid: You don't push and shove cause somebody could fall down and get hurt.

Miss Lora: Kids are watching and listening all the time, we forget that. We think ohhh they're just lost in their own world — no they're not.

Lindsey: Etiquette expert and author of, "Y'all Are Rude," Miss Lora explains that kids mimic your every move.

Miss Lora: They're constantly paying attention. They're trying to figure out who they're gonna be when they grow up, and honey they're gonna be you. So if you're pushing and shoving everybody else and going, "I'm busy I gotta get you know get my way through there" that's who they're gonna turn out to be.

Lindsey: Our second courteous crumb snatcher:

Kid: Say please. Say thank you.

Miss Lora: There's actually a scientific reason why adults should stop being rude rude rude and they need to say thank you all the time.Scientists have proven that when you actually look at something, you observe it, you change it. It's quantum physics and that means that anything you put your focus on is gonna get bigger and better.

Lindsey: So you're telling me I should just wake up and say thank you for the day, thank you for the Starbucks, thank you for my job, another payday.

Miss Lora: Absolutely.

Lindsey: And the third piece of ankle-biter etiquette: be nice.

Toddler: (mumbles) be nice

Kid: Everybody knows the golden rule right? Treat others the—the way you wanna be treated.

Miss Lora: Remember, what you put out into the world is what you're gonna get back. And every opportunity you have to do something nice for someone is a chance to make the world a better place. And sometimes just smiling at somebody, just seeing somebody give them a big old smile.

Lindsey: (gives a big smile)

Both: (laughter)

Lindsey: See how you changed! That's it, will you please come down the slide with me?

Miss Lora: I would love to! Thank you!

Lindsey: Oh this is so awesome, your etiquette is on point. Let's go! Tips from tots on being your best on the breakdown.

Miss Lora on The List TV Show with Lindsey Granger: No Rude Rules of Regifting!

Lindsey: Regifting is a perfect save when you need a present but it can easily backfire and make you look like a jerk. Like this classic Seinfeld episode.

Seinfeld ep: He recycled this gift. He's a regifter!

Lindsey: You could really offend somebody. If it's your boss that gave it to you and you give it to your other boss.

Miss Lora: Or family now its even more offending.

Lindsey: Miss Lora, etiquette expert and author of, "Y'all Are Rude," has some key advice on how not to get caught.

Miss Lora: The first thing is don't give a gift that makes no sense. Think about the person, you know, you don't want to give a gardening tool to somebody who lives in an apartment.

Lindsey: Make sure you can actually envision the person using the gift you give them. Ok so what's your next rule for regifting.

Miss Lora: Ok well don't regift in the same circle of friends. The bottom line is that when you get a gift and the first thing in your thought is, "that is not staying with me," put a note on it so that you know who gave it to you.

Lindsey: Miss Lora says that the note will help you avoid giving it back to the same person who gave it to you. What's your final regifting no-no?

Miss Lora: Don't put it in the original wrapping. I mean I can't believe people even save wrapping. It gets torn up, and the tape, and the whole— it's like please.

Lindsey: Cause you're just being kind of cheap if you can't just go buy a $3.99 bag. You didn't pay for the gift.

Miss Lora: Well the bottom line is like a big red flag that says, "look, this is a regifting thing!" You know, if you're trying to get away with something, you just blew that.

Lindsey: And if you're wondering what the best items to regift are.

Miss Lora: It is not rude to give gift cards or even cash.

Lindsey: And she means gift cards that were given to you.

Miss Lora: Seriously, everybody needs a little help and they really appreciate it. And the thing is they make them nice now like you can even take them and put them in a little wrapper and they're so cute, you know.

Lindsey: Just make sure there's a full balance on that card.

Regifting: the right way. On the to-do list

Baking Soda Tips

Baking Soda Tip #1

Now, here's another tip. Bad language often goes with bad breath but I've got a solution for that: baking soda, hon, really. Just take about a half teaspoon of this with a little glass of water to wash your mouth out because you probably need to. Swallow it down and you'll have sweet breath to impress some nice girl. Well, at least, til another cuss word comes flyin' out of your mouth. Mmhmm. Until next time, mind your manners, y'all.

Baking Soda Tip #2

Now if you want to make a good first impression every time, all you need is baking soda, hon, really. Just sprinkle a little bit of this in your facial soap and then gently scrub your face. It will get rid of all that grease and dead skin. You'll look all smooth and shiny and pretty and make a wonderful impression on your date - unless you start yodeling. Until next time, mind your manners, y'all.

Baking Soda Tip #3

So, if you'd like your vegetables to be as fresh as you are, gentlemen, there's a perfect way to do that: baking soda, hon, really. You just sprinkle a little bit of this on your fruit and veggies and then you can scrub off all those pesticides and that waxy residue. And then they'll be perfect for making a nice dinner for your new date. Until next time, mind your manners, y'all.

Baking Soda Tip #4

Now if you want to make the perfect wedding present, you tape that gift certificate to a bag of baking soda, hon, really. It's perfect for scrubbing all those greasy pots and pans and you want to get your husband in the kitchen doing dishes as early in the marriage as you can. Train him right, girls! Until next time, mind your manners, y'all.

Baking Soda Tip #5

If you have a boss who's giving you an ulcer, I have a simple solution for you – baking soda, hon, really! You just take about a half a teaspoon of it in a glass of water with a valium and that'll calm everything right down. Of course, tuning out your boss' voice - that just takes practice. Until next time, mind your manners, y'all!

Baking Soda Tip #6

Now if you've got a foot problem, Miss Lora has the solution – baking soda, hon, really! If you've got toenail fungus or athlete's foot, just mix a quarter cup of baking soda with an eighth of a cup of hydrogen peroxide in a small basin. Soak your doggies every night for a week or two and they'll be good as new. Until next time, mind your manners, y'all!

Soda Tip #7

And if you're looking for some bonus points, you could go on over to her house and scrub her kitchen with baking soda, hon, really! Cuz nothing says you're more manly than going over to your woman's Momma's house and scrubbing her kitchen sinks. And when your girl sees those muscles just glistenin' with sweat – oh honey, big plans ahead! Until next time, mind your manners, y'all!

Baking Soda Tip #8

Let's be honest. Maybe the real reason why you're not gettin' in the tub is cuz the kids have been in it and it's filthy with that big old black ring. You need to give them baking soda, hon, really so they can clean it out for you! Use it cuz it's organic, it's healthy and it accomplishes several things. First of all, they get exercise cuz they're in there just scrubbin' away. Then you give them 50 cents which they can run out and use for the ice cream truck! Ding dong, ding dong! And while they're out there gettin' that ice cream, you hop in the tub! Until next time, mind your manners, y'all!

Baking Soda Tip #9

Well, the only part I didn't like about swimming, besides the drowning part, was that it made you look like an alien. Your hair would be puffed out to here and all green. But I have the perfect solution for that - baking soda, hon, really! Just put a little bit in your favorite shampoo. It'll strip that nasty old chlorine out of your hair and leave it all shiny and pretty and you'll be ready for your date with your crush! Until next time, mind your manners, y'all!

Baking Soda Tip #10

Now, if you want to make your automobile better, I got a solution for that: baking soda, hon, really! You just mix some water with it and make a paste. Then you spread it all over your battery connectors and cables and it will bubble up and clean off that nasty old corrosion without any scrubbing at all. Until next time, mind your manners, y'all.

Baking Soda Tip #11

Well, if you'd like to make your life better, all you need is baking soda, hon, really. Just take about a half a teaspoon of baking soda and put it in any recipe of your baked goods. It'll make them rise better and taste better and then you can convince yourself that you're doing somethin' healthy while you're eatin' all that crap. Until next time, mind your manners, y'all.

Baking Soda Tip #12

Now, if you'd like to do something nice for your dog, I've got a solution for that: baking soda, hon, really. Just put some of this in their doggy shampoo and you know those little itchy hot spots they get? It'll clear them right up and their fur will be perfect for petting after that. But keep 'em on the floor and off the dining room table and chairs, I'm beggin' you. Until next time, mind your manners y'all.

Baking Soda Tip #13

Now, if you want to do something nice for your kitties, all you need is baking soda, hon, really. Just take about a cup of this – oh, what am I talkin' about, you just need to dump the whole HUGE bag of it into that kitty litter box and pray for the best. Really. Until next time, mind your manners, y'all.

Baking Soda Tip #14

It is a stressful situation but Miss Lora has the perfect solution for it: a hot bath and baking soda, hon, really! It's organic, it's healthy and it's cheap! It's a great detoxer, gets rid of all that electromagnetic energy and clears out your auric field. I don't know what that means but it works, whatever. Anyway, some people just like to use a little bit of it but I say just dump it all in there. And if you mix it with Epsom Salts, you get these bubbles. So then when you're sittin' in the tub, you get all these little tingles. Miss Lora is a big believer that life is hard. We need to get our tingles wherever we can – especially if they're legal and cheap! Until next time, mind your manners, y'all!

Baking Soda Tip #15

But if you're cookin' in the car, the grease stains on the upholstery are horrendous so you need baking soda, hon, really. Just sprinkle a little bit on the spots, it will lift that grease right up. Then you take an old toothbrush and scrap it all away and it's good as new. At least, until she makes the next batch of doughnuts. Until next time, mind your manners, y'all.

Baking Soda Tip #16

Well, if you ladies want to look pretty all the time, I've got the perfect solution for you: baking soda, hon, really. You just sprinkle a little bit of it on the toothpaste on your toothbrush and your pearly whites will be gleamin' so much, nobody will even notice if you're fat. Really. Until next time, mind yer manners, y'all!

Baking Soda Tip #17

Now ladies, you need to make sure you have the most important thing in your purse which is a zip lock baggy of mother's little helper: baking soda, hon, really. Cause if you or the kids get sunburned, you could just mix it with water and make a little paste and very gently put it on all those burned places. By the time you get home and rinse it off, the red will be completely gone! Really. Until next time, mind your manners, y'all.

Baking Soda Tip #18

Now, if you gentlemen would like to make that time on the couch a little nicer, I've got a solution for that: baking soda, hon, really. All ya gotta do is pick up them couch cushions and get all those nasty pizza crusts and Twinkie wrappers out of there. Then sprinkle a little bit of baking soda on the bottom. Vacuum it all up and it will smell good as new. And with all that cleanin', it might earn you some extra points with the Mrs. and get you off the couch that much quicker. See, that's the thing about baking soda. Whatever interesting things you do, it makes it all fine. Until next time, mind your manners, y'all.

Baking Soda Tip #19

Now if you need to decontaminate your clothes, you just need baking soda, hon – really! Just add half a cup to your washer and it acts as a laundry booster to make your clothes cleaner, your whites brighter and it can even erase the stain of betrayal. Really. Until next time, mind your manners, y'all!

Baking Soda Tip #20

Now what does cover the stink is - baking soda, hon, really. You just sprinkle a little bit of this in those funky tennis shoes and shake out the excess and they'll be smelling fine in no time. Until next time, mind your manners, y'all.

Baking Soda Tip #21

Well, we can't do much about the fees for now but you can keep your luggage in better shape with baking soda, hon, really! Just make a paste of it with some water and use a scrub brush to get all those cooties off of it cuz between the TSA and the tarmac, you have no idea where it's been! Until next time, mind your manners, y'all!

YOUR BAKING SODA TIPS

YOUR BAKING SODA TIPS

www.ingramcontent.com/pod-product-compliance
Lightning Source LLC
Chambersburg PA
CBHW070519030426
42337CB00016B/2022